The 30-Minute Pescatarian
Cookbook

TABLE OF CONTENTS

TABLE OF CONTENTS

TABLE OF CONTENTS

Asparagus 'n' Shrimp with Angel Hair

| Cooking Information | | | | |

A. Ingredients

3 ounces uncooked angel hair pasta

1/2 pound uncooked shrimp, peeled and deveined

1/4 teaspoon salt

1/8 teaspoon crushed red pepper flakes

2 tablespoons olive oil, divided

8 fresh asparagus spears, trimmed

1/2 cup sliced fresh mushrooms

1/4 cup chopped seeded tomato, peeled

4 garlic cloves, minced

2 teaspoons chopped green onion

1/2 cup white wine or chicken broth

1-1/2 teaspoons minced fresh basil

1-1/2 teaspoons minced fresh oregano

B. Instructions

Step 1: Cook pasta according to package directions.

Step 2: Meanwhile, sprinkle shrimp with salt and pepper flakes. In a large skillet or wok, heat 1 tablespoon oil over medium-high heat. Add shrimp; stir-fry until pink, 2-3 minutes. Remove; keep warm.

Step 3: In same skillet, stir-fry the next 5 ingredients in remaining oil until vegetables are crisp-tender, about 5 minutes. Add wine and seasonings. Return shrimp to pan.

Drain pasta; add to shrimp mixture and toss gently.

Step 4: Cook and stir until heated through, 1-2 minutes. Sprinkle with Parmesan cheese. Serve with lemon wedges.

C. Nutrition Facts

1-3/4 cups:

Calories: 488 Total Fat: 19g Total Carbohydrates: 41g Protein: 29g

Buttery Grilled Shrimp

Cooking Information				

A. Ingredients

1/2 cup butter, melted

3 tablespoons lemon juice

2 teaspoons chili powder

1 teaspoon ground ginger

1/4 teaspoon salt

2 pounds uncooked shrimp (16-20 per pound), peeled and deveined

B. Instructions

Step 1: In a small bowl, combine the first 5 ingredients; set aside 1/4 cup. Thread shrimp onto 8 metal or soaked wooden skewers.

Step 2: Grill shrimp, covered, over medium heat 3-5 minutes on each side or until shrimp turn pink, basting occasionally with butter mixture.

Step 3: Remove from grill; brush with reserved butter mixture.

C. Nutrition Facts

1 skewer:

Calories: 201

Total Fat: 13g

Total Carbohydrates: 2g

Protein: 19g

Fajita-Style Shrimp and Grits

Cooking Information |

A. Ingredients

1 cup stone-ground grits
4 cups chicken or vegetable broth
1 pound peeled, deveined shrimp
1 tablespoon olive oil
1 onion, sliced
1 red bell pepper, sliced
1 yellow bell pepper, sliced
1 tablespoon chili powder
1 teaspoon ground cumin
1 teaspoon garlic, minced
2 limes, halved

B. Instructions

Step 1: Bring the grits and broth to a boil in a large sauce pan. Reduce to a simmer and cook for 15 minutes, stirring regularly until thickened.

Step 2: Season the shrimp with salt and pepper. Heat the olive oil in a skillet over medium high. Add the shrimp and cook for 2 minutes. Transfer the cooked shrimp to a plate.

Step 3: Add the onion and peppers to the skillet and cook until tender, about 5 minutes. Stir in the chili powder, cumin and garlic and cook for 30 seconds more.

Step 4: Return the shrimp to the skillet and squeeze fresh lime juice over everything. Stir for a minute to coat.

Step 5: Divide the grits between two bowls and top with the fajita-style shrimp and vegetables. Serve with lime wedges.

C. Nutrition Facts

Per serving:
Calories: 390 Total Fat: 7g Carbohydrates: 54g Protein: 27g

Pretzel-Crusted Catfish

Cooking Information					

A. Ingredients

4 catfish fillets (6 ounces each)

1/2 teaspoon salt

1/2 teaspoon pepper

2 large eggs

1/3 cup Dijon mustard

2 tablespoons 2% milk

1/2 cup all-purpose flour

4 cups honey mustard miniature pretzels, coarsely crushed

Oil for frying

Lemon slices, optional

B. Instructions

Step 1: Sprinkle catfish with salt and pepper. Whisk the eggs, mustard and milk in a shallow bowl.

Step 2: Place flour and pretzels in separate shallow bowls. Coat fillets with flour, then dip in egg mixture and coat with pretzels.

Step 3: Heat 1/4 in. oil to 375° in an electric skillet. Fry fillets, a few at a time, until fish flakes easily with a fork, 3-4 minutes on each side.

Step 4: Drain on paper towels. Serve with lemon slices if desired.

C. Nutrition Facts

1 fillet:

Calories: 610

Total Fat: 31g

Total Carbohydrates: 44g

Protein: 33g

Garlic-Herb Salmon Sliders

Cooking Information

A. Ingredients

1/3 cup panko bread crumbs

4 teaspoons finely chopped shallot

2 teaspoons snipped fresh dill

1 tablespoon prepared horseradish

1 large egg, beaten

1/4 teaspoon salt

1/8 teaspoon pepper

1 pound salmon fillet, skin removed, cut into 1-inch cubes

8 whole wheat dinner rolls, split and toasted

1/4 cup reduced-fat garlic-herb spreadable cheese

8 small lettuce leaves

B. Instructions

Step 1: In a large bowl, combine the first 7 ingredients.

Step 2: Place salmon in a food processor; pulse until coarsely chopped, and add to bread crumb mixture. Mix lightly but thoroughly. Shape into eight 1/2-in.-thick patties.

Step 3: On a lightly greased grill rack, grill burgers, covered, over medium heat or broil 4 in. from heat until a thermometer reads 160°, 3-4 minutes on each side.

Step 4: Serve on rolls with spreadable cheese and lettuce.

C. Nutrition Facts

2 sliders:

Calories: 442

Total Fat: 17g

Total Carbohydrates: 42g

Protein: 30g

Feta Tomato–Basil Fish

| Cooking Information | | | | |

A. Ingredients

1/3 cup chopped onion

1 garlic clove, minced

2 teaspoons olive oil

1 can (14-1/2 ounces) Italian diced tomatoes, drained

1-1/2 teaspoons minced fresh basil or 1/2 teaspoon dried basil

1 pound walleye, bass or other white fish fillets

4 ounces crumbled feta cheese

B. Instructions

Step 1: In a saucepan, saute onion and garlic in oil until tender.

Step 2: Add tomatoes and basil. Bring to a boil. Reduce heat; simmer, uncovered, for 5 minutes.

Step 3: Meanwhile, broil fish 4-6 in. from the heat for 5-6 minutes.

Step 4: Top each fillet with tomato mixture and cheese.

Broil 5-7 minutes longer or until fish just begins to flake easily with a fork.

C. Nutrition Facts

1 serving:
Calories: 241
Total Fat: 8g
Total Carbohydrates: 12g
Protein: 28g

Avocado Crab Boats

| Cooking Information | | | | |

A. Ingredients

5 medium ripe avocados, peeled and halved

1/2 cup mayonnaise

2 tablespoons lemon juice

2 cans (6 ounces each) lump crabmeat, drained

4 tablespoons chopped fresh cilantro, divided

2 tablespoons minced chives

1 serrano pepper, seeded and minced

1 tablespoon capers, drained

1/4 teaspoon pepper

1 cup shredded pepper jack cheese

1/2 teaspoon paprika

Lemon wedges

B. Instructions

Step 1: Preheat broiler. Place 2 avocado halves in a large bowl; mash lightly with a fork. Add mayonnaise and lemon juice; mix until well blended.

Step 2: Stir in crab, 3 tablespoons cilantro, chives, serrano pepper, capers and pepper. Spoon into remaining avocado halves.

Step 3: Transfer to a 15x10x1-in. baking pan. Sprinkle with cheese and paprika. Broil 4-5 in. from heat until cheese is melted, 3-5 minutes.

Sprinkle with remaining cilantro; serve with lemon wedges.

C. Nutrition Facts

1 filled avocado half:

Calories: 325

Total Fat: 28g

Total Carbohydrates: 8g

Protein: 13g

New Orleans–Style Spicy Shrimp

Cooking Information

A. Ingredients

3 medium lemons, sliced
2/3 cup butter, cubed
1/2 cup ketchup
1/4 cup Worcestershire sauce
2 tablespoons seafood seasoning
2 tablespoons chili garlic sauce
2 tablespoons Louisiana-style hot sauce
1 tablespoon Italian salad dressing mix
4 pounds uncooked shell-on shrimp
2 bay leaves
French bread

B. Instructions

Step 1: Preheat oven to 350°. In a microwave-safe bowl, combine the first 8 ingredients.

Step 2: Microwave, covered, on high 2-3 minutes or until butter is melted; stir until blended.

Step 3: Divide shrimp and bay leaves between 2 ungreased 13x9-in. baking dishes. Add half of the lemon mixture to each dish; toss to combine.

Step 4: Bake, uncovered, 20-25 minutes or until shrimp turn pink, stirring halfway. Remove bay leaves. Serve with bread.

C. Nutrition Facts

1 cup (calculated without bread):
Calories: 242
Total Fat: 12g
Total Carbohydrates: 7g
Protein: 25g

Fish and Fries

| Cooking Information | | | | |

A. Ingredients

1 pound potatoes (about 2 medium)

2 tablespoons olive oil

1/4 teaspoon pepper

1/3 cup all-purpose flour

1/4 teaspoon pepper

1 large egg

2 tablespoons water

2/3 cup crushed cornflakes

1 tablespoon grated Parmesan cheese

1/8 teaspoon cayenne pepper

1 pound haddock or cod fillets

Tartar sauce, optional

B. Instructions

Step 1: Preheat oven to 425°. Peel and cut potatoes lengthwise into 1/2-in.-thick slices; cut slices into 1/2-in.-thick sticks.

Step 2: In a large bowl, toss potatoes with oil and pepper. Transfer to a 15x10x1-in. baking pan coated with cooking spray. Bake, uncovered, 25-30 minutes or until golden brown and crisp, stirring once.

Step 3: Meanwhile, in a shallow bowl, mix flour and pepper. In another shallow bowl, whisk egg with water. In a third bowl, toss cornflakes with cheese and cayenne. Dip fish in flour mixture to coat both sides; shake off excess. Dip in egg mixture, then in cornflake mixture, patting to help coating adhere.

Step 4: Place on a baking sheet coated with cooking spray. Bake 10-12 minutes or until fish just begins to flake easily with a fork. Serve with potatoes and, if desired, tartar sauce.

C. Nutrition Facts

Per serving:
Calories: 376 Total Fat: 9g Total Carbohydrates: 44g Protein: 28g

Sheet-Pan Chipotle-Lime Shrimp Bake

Cooking Information

A. Ingredients

1-1/2 pounds baby red potatoes, cut into 3/4-inch cubes

1 tablespoon extra virgin olive oil

3/4 teaspoon sea salt, divided

3 medium limes

1/4 cup unsalted butter, melted

1 teaspoon ground chipotle pepper

1/2 pound fresh asparagus, trimmed

1/2 pound Broccolini or broccoli, cut into small florets

1 pound uncooked shrimp (16-20 per pound), peeled and deveined

2 tablespoons minced fresh cilantro

B. Instructions

Step 1: Preheat oven to 400°. Place potatoes in a greased 15x10x1-in. baking pan; drizzle with olive oil. Sprinkle with 1/4 teaspoon sea salt; stir to combine. Bake for 30 minutes.

Step 2: Meanwhile, squeeze 1/3 cup juice from limes, reserving fruit. Combine the lime juice, melted butter, chipotle and remaining 1/2 teaspoon sea salt.

Step 3: Remove pan from the oven; stir potatoes. Arrange asparagus, Broccolini, shrimp and reserved limes on top of potatoes. Pour lime juice mixture over vegetables and shrimp.

Step 4: Bake until shrimp turn pink and vegetables are tender, about 10 minutes longer. Sprinkle with minced fresh cilantro.

C. Nutrition Facts

Per serving:
Calories: 394
Total Fat: 17g
Total Carbohydrates: 41g
Protein: 25g

Lemon Shrimp with Parmesan Rice

| Cooking Information | | | | |

A. Ingredients

2 cups chicken broth

2 cups uncooked instant rice

1 pound uncooked medium shrimp, peeled and deveined

1/2 cup chopped green onions

2 tablespoons butter

2 tablespoons olive oil

2 teaspoons minced garlic

3 tablespoons lemon juice

1/4 teaspoon pepper

1/2 cup grated Parmesan cheese

2 tablespoons minced fresh parsley

B. Instructions

Step 1: In a small saucepan, bring broth to a boil. Stir in rice; cover and remove from the heat. Let stand for 5 minutes.

Step 2: Meanwhile, in a large cast-iron or other heavy skillet, cook shrimp and onions in butter and oil over medium heat until shrimp turn pink, 4-5 minutes.

Step 3: Add garlic; cook 1 minute longer. Stir in lemon juice and pepper. Stir cheese and parsley into rice; serve with shrimp

C. Nutrition Facts

1 cup shrimp with 3/4 cup rice:

Calories: 438

Total Fat: 17g

Total Carbohydrates: 43g

Protein: 27g

Tuna Steak On Fettuccine

A. Ingredients

2 tuna steaks (6oz each)

8oz fettuccine pasta

2 tablespoons olive oil

3 cloves garlic, minced

¼ cup dry white wine

1 cup cherry tomatoes, halved

1 lemon, juiced

¼ cup fresh parsley, chopped

Salt and pepper to taste

Grated Parmesan cheese (optional)

B. Instructions

Step 1: Bring a large pot of salted water to a boil. Cook fettuccine according to package directions. Drain and set aside.

Step 2: Pat tuna steaks dry and season both sides with salt and pepper. Heat oil in a large skillet over medium-high heat. When hot, add tuna and cook for about 3-4 minutes per side until opaque and flakes easily. Transfer to a plate and cover with foil.

Step 3: To the skillet, add garlic and cook for 30 seconds until fragrant. Deglaze pan with white wine. Let reduce slightly, then add cherry tomatoes and lemon juice. Cook for 2-3 minutes until tomatoes start to burst.

Step 4: Add the cooked fettuccine and parsley to the skillet and toss everything together. Top fettuccine with the flaked tuna steaks. Garnish with Parmesan if desired.

C. Nutrition Facts

Per serving:

Calories: 640 Total Fat: 16g Total Carbohydrates: 71g Protein: 48g

Cajun Shrimp Skillet

Cooking Information |

A. Ingredients

3 tablespoons butter
2 garlic cloves, minced
1/2 cup amber beer or beef broth
1 teaspoon Worcestershire sauce
1 teaspoon pepper
1/2 teaspoon salt
1/2 teaspoon dried thyme
1/2 teaspoon dried rosemary, crushed
1/2 teaspoon crushed red pepper flakes
1/4 teaspoon cayenne pepper
1/8 teaspoon dried oregano
1 pound uncooked large shrimp, peeled and deveined
Hot cooked grits, optional

B. Instructions

Step 1: In a large cast-iron or other heavy skillet, heat butter over medium-high heat. Step 2: Add garlic; cook and stir 1 minute. Stir in beer, Worcestershire sauce and seasonings; bring to a boil.
Step 3: Add shrimp; cook until shrimp turn pink, 3-4 minutes, stirring occasionally.
If desired, serve over grits.

C. Nutrition Facts

1/2 cup (calculated without grits):
Calories: 186 Total Fat: 10g Total Carbohydrates: 3g Protein: 19g

Cajun Boil on the Grill

| Cooking Information | | | | |

A. Ingredients

1 package (20 ounces) refrigerated red potato wedges

2 salmon fillets (6 ounces each), halved

3/4 pound uncooked shrimp (31-40 per pound), peeled and deveined

1/2 pound summer sausage, cubed

2 medium ears sweet corn, halved

2 tablespoons olive oil

1 teaspoon seafood seasoning

1/2 teaspoon salt

1/4 teaspoon pepper

1 medium lemon, cut into 4 wedges

B. Instructions

Step 1: Divide potatoes, salmon, shrimp, sausage and corn among four pieces of heavy-duty foil (about 18x12-in. rectangles).

Step 2: Drizzle with oil; sprinkle with seasonings. Squeeze lemon juice over top; place squeezed wedges in packets. Fold foil around mixture, sealing tightly.

Step 3: Grill, covered, over medium heat 12-15 minutes or until fish just begins to flake easily with a fork, shrimp turn pink and potatoes are tender.

Open foil carefully to allow steam to escape.

C. Nutrition Facts

Per serving:
Calories: 509
Total Fat: 30g
Total Carbohydrates: 21g
Protein: 40g

Grilled Lobster Tails

| Cooking Information | | | | |

A. Ingredients

6 frozen lobster tails (8 to 10 ounces each), thawed

3/4 cup olive oil

3 tablespoons minced fresh chives

3 garlic cloves, minced

1/2 teaspoon salt

1/2 teaspoon pepper

B. Instructions

Step 1: Using scissors, cut 3 to 4 lengthwise slits in underside of tail to loosen shell slightly.

Step 2: Cut top of lobster shell lengthwise down the center with scissors, leaving tail fin intact. Cut shell at an angle away from the center of the tail at base of tail fin. Loosen meat from shell, keeping the fin end attached; lift meat and lay over shell.

Step 3: In a small bowl, combine the remaining ingredients; spoon over lobster meat. Cover and refrigerate for 20 minutes.

Step 4: Place lobster tails, meat side up, on grill rack. Grill, covered, over medium heat until meat is opaque, 10-12 minutes

C. Nutrition Facts

1 lobster tail:
Calories: 446
Total Fat: 29g
Total Carbohydrates: 2g
Protein: 43g

Scallops in Sage Cream

| Cooking Information | | | | |

A. Ingredients

1-1/2 pounds sea scallops
1/4 teaspoon salt
1/8 teaspoon pepper
3 tablespoons olive oil, divided
1/2 cup chopped shallots
3/4 cup heavy whipping cream
6 fresh sage leaves, thinly sliced
Hot cooked pasta, optional

B. Instructions

Step 1: Sprinkle scallops with salt and pepper.
Step 2: In a large skillet, cook scallops in 2 tablespoons oil until firm and opaque, 1-1/2-2 minutes on each side. Remove and keep warm.
Step 3: In the same skillet, saute shallots in remaining 1 tablespoon oil until tender. Add cream; bring to a boil.
Step 4: Cook and stir for 30 seconds or until slightly thickened.
Return scallops to the pan; heat through. Stir in sage.
Serve with pasta if desired.

C. Nutrition Facts

Per serving:
Calories: 408
Total Fat: 28g
Total Carbohydrates: 9g
Protein: 30g

Shrimp Pasta Alfredo

| Cooking Information | | | | |

A. Ingredients

3 cups uncooked bow tie pasta

2 cups frozen peas

1 pound peeled and deveined cooked medium shrimp, tails removed

1 jar (15 ounces) Alfredo sauce

1/4 cup shredded Parmesan cheese

B. Instructions

Step 1: In a Dutch oven, cook pasta according to package directions, adding peas during the last 3 minutes of cooking; drain and return to pan.

Step 2: Stir in shrimp and sauce; heat through over medium heat, stirring occasionally. Sprinkle with cheese.

C. Nutrition Facts

2 cups:

Calories: 545

Total Fat: 16g

Total Carbohydrates: 60g

Protein: 41g

Classic Crab Cakes

| Cooking Information | | | | | |

A. Ingredients

1 pound fresh or canned crabmeat, drained, flaked and cartilage removed
2 to 2-1/2 cups soft bread crumbs
1 large egg, beaten
3/4 cup mayonnaise
1/3 cup each chopped celery, green pepper and onion
2 teaspoons lemon juice
1 tablespoon seafood seasoning
1 tablespoon minced fresh parsley
1 teaspoon Worcestershire sauce
1 teaspoon prepared mustard
1/4 teaspoon pepper
1/8 teaspoon hot pepper sauce
Optional: 2 to 4 tablespoons canola oil and lemon wedges

B. Instructions

Step 1: In a large bowl, combine the crab, bread crumbs, egg, mayonnaise, vegetables, juice and seasonings.
Step 2: Shape mixture into 8 patties. Broil the patties in a cast-iron or other ovenproof skillet or, if desired, cook the patties in skillet on stovetop in oil; cook for 4 minutes on each side or until golden brown.
If desired, serve with lemon.

C. Nutrition Facts

1 crab cake:
Calories: 282 Total Fat: 22g Total Carbohydrates: 7g Protein: 14g

Asian Salmon Tacos

| Cooking Information | | | | |

A. Ingredients

1 pound salmon fillet, skin removed, cut into 1-inch cubes

2 tablespoons hoisin sauce

1 tablespoon olive oil

Shredded lettuce

8 corn tortillas (6 inches), warmed

1-1/2 teaspoons black sesame seeds

Mango salsa, optional

B. Instructions

Step 1: Toss salmon with hoisin sauce. In a large nonstick skillet, heat oil over medium-high heat.

Step 2: Cook salmon for 3-5 minutes or until it begins to flake easily with a fork, turning gently to brown all sides.

Step 3: Serve salmon and lettuce in tortillas; sprinkle with sesame seeds.

If desired, top with salsa.

C. Nutrition Facts

2 tacos:

Calories: 335

Total Fat: 16g

Total Carbohydrates: 25g

Protein: 22g

Stir-Fried Shrimp and Mushrooms

| Cooking Information | | | | |

A. Ingredients

4 garlic cloves, minced

2 teaspoons canola oil

1 pound uncooked shrimp (31-40 per pound), peeled and deveined

3 cups sliced fresh mushrooms

1 cup sliced green onions

1/4 cup chicken broth

Hot cooked rice

Lemon slices

B. Instructions

Step 1: In a large skillet or wok, saute garlic in oil for 1 minute.

Step 2: Add the shrimp, mushrooms and onions; stir-fry for 1 minute.

Step 3: Stir in the broth; cook 2 minutes longer or until shrimp turn pink.

Serve with rice; garnish with lemon.

C. Nutrition Facts

Per serving:
Calories: 132
Total Fat: 3g
Total Carbohydrates: 5g
Protein: 20g

Basil–Lemon Crab Linguine

Cooking Information

A. Ingredients

1 package (9 ounces) refrigerated linguine

1/3 cup butter, cubed

1 jalapeno pepper, seeded and finely chopped

1 garlic clove, minced

1 teaspoon grated lemon zest

3 tablespoons lemon juice

2 cans (6 ounces each) lump crabmeat, drained

1/4 cup loosely packed basil leaves, thinly sliced

1/2 teaspoon sea salt

1/4 teaspoon freshly ground pepper

B. Instructions

Step 1: Cook linguine according to package directions.

Step 2: Meanwhile, in a large skillet, heat butter over medium heat. Add jalapeno and garlic; cook and stir 1-2 minutes or until tender.

Step 3: Stir in lemon zest and juice. Add crab; heat through, stirring gently.

Step 3: Drain linguine; add to skillet. Sprinkle with basil, salt and pepper; toss to combine.

C. Nutrition Facts

1-1/4 cups:
Calories: 392
Total Fat: 18g
Total Carbohydrates: 35g
Protein: 23g

Crab-Topped Fish Fillets

| Cooking Information | | | | |

A. Ingredients

4 sole or cod fillets, or fish fillets of your choice (6 ounces each)

1 can (6 ounces) crabmeat, drained and flaked, or 1 cup imitation crabmeat, chopped

1/2 cup grated Parmesan cheese

1/2 cup mayonnaise

1 teaspoon lemon juice

1/3 cup slivered almonds, toasted

Paprika, optional

B. Instructions

Step 1: Preheat oven to 350°. Place fillets in a greased 13x9-in. baking pan. Bake, uncovered, until fish flakes easily with a fork, 18-22 minutes.

Step 2: Meanwhile, in a large bowl, combine the crab, cheese, mayonnaise and lemon juice.

Step 3: Drain cooking juices from baking dish; spoon crab mixture over fillets. Broil 4-5 in. from the heat until topping is lightly browned, about 5 minutes.

Step 4: Sprinkle with almonds and, if desired, paprika.

C. Nutrition Facts

1 fillet:
Calories: 429
Total Fat: 31g
Total Carbohydrates: 3g
Protein: 33g

Pesto Shrimp Pasta

Cooking Information

A. Ingredients

8 ounces uncooked spaghetti

3 tablespoons olive oil, divided

1 cup loosely packed fresh basil leaves

1/4 cup lemon juice

2 garlic cloves, peeled

1/2 teaspoon salt

1 pound fresh asparagus, trimmed and cut into 2-inch pieces

3/4 pound uncooked medium shrimp, peeled and deveined

1/8 teaspoon crushed red pepper flakes

B. Instructions

Step 1: Cook spaghetti according to package directions. Meanwhile, in a blender, combine 1 tablespoon oil, basil, lemon juice, garlic and salt; cover and process until smooth.

Step 2: In a large skillet, saute asparagus in remaining oil until crisp-tender. Add shrimp and pepper flakes. Cook and stir until shrimp turn pink, 2-4 minutes.

Step 3: Drain spaghetti; place in a large bowl. Add basil mixture; toss to coat. Add shrimp mixture and mix well.

C. Nutrition Facts

1 cup:
Calories: 393
Total Fat: 12g
Total Carbohydrates: 47g
Protein: 23g

A recipe has no soul unless you bring it to life.

Orzo Shrimp Stew

Cooking Information |

A. Ingredients

2-1/2 cups reduced-sodium chicken broth
5 cups fresh broccoli florets
1 can (14-1/2 ounces) diced tomatoes, undrained
1 cup uncooked orzo
1 pound uncooked shrimp (31-40 per pound), peeled and deveined
1/4 teaspoon salt
1/4 teaspoon pepper
2 teaspoons dried basil
2 tablespoons butter

B. Instructions

Step 1: Bring broth to a boil in a Dutch oven.
Add the broccoli, tomatoes and orzo. Reduce heat; simmer, uncovered, for 5 minutes, stirring occasionally.
Step 2: Add the shrimp, salt and pepper.
Cover and cook for 4-5 minutes or until shrimp turn pink and orzo is tender. Stir in basil and butter.

C. Nutrition Facts

1-3/4 cups:
Calories: 387
Total Fat: 8g
Total Carbohydrates: 48g
Protein: 30g

Seared Scallops with Citrus Herb Sauce

Cooking Information					

A. Ingredients

3/4 pound sea scallops

1/4 teaspoon salt

1/4 teaspoon pepper

1/8 teaspoon paprika

3 tablespoons butter, divided

1 garlic clove, minced

2 tablespoons dry sherry or chicken broth

1 tablespoon lemon juice

1/8 teaspoon minced fresh oregano

1/8 teaspoon minced fresh tarragon

B. Instructions

Step 1: Pat scallops dry with paper towels; sprinkle with salt, pepper and paprika. In a large skillet, heat 2 tablespoons butter over medium-high heat.

Step 2: Add scallops; sear for 1-2 minutes on each side or until golden brown and firm. Remove from the skillet; keep warm.

Step 3: Wipe skillet clean if necessary. Saute garlic in remaining butter until tender; stir in sherry.

Step 4: Cook until liquid is almost evaporated; stir in the remaining ingredients. Serve with scallops.

C. Nutrition Facts

3 scallops with 1-1/2 teaspoons sauce:

Calories: 314

Total Fat: 18g

Total Carbohydrates: 6g

Protein: 29g

Shrimp Puttanesca

Cooking Information

A. Ingredients

2 tablespoons olive oil, divided
1 pound uncooked shrimp, peeled and deveined
3/4 to 1 teaspoon crushed red pepper flakes, divided
1/4 teaspoon salt
1 small onion, chopped
2 to 3 anchovy fillets, finely chopped
3 garlic cloves, minced
2 cups grape tomatoes or small cherry tomatoes
1/2 cup dry white wine or vegetable broth
1/3 cup pitted Greek olives, coarsely chopped
2 teaspoons drained capers
Sugar to taste
Chopped fresh Italian parsley

B. Instructions

Step 1: In a large skillet, heat 1 tablespoon oil; saute shrimp with 1/2 teaspoon pepper flakes until shrimp turn pink, 2-3 minutes. Stir in salt; remove from pan.

Step 2: In same pan, heat remaining oil over medium heat; saute onion until tender, about 2 minutes. Add anchovies, garlic and remaining pepper flakes; cook and stir until fragrant, about 1 minute. Stir in tomatoes, wine, olives and capers; bring to a boil. Reduce heat; simmer, uncovered, until tomatoes are softened and mixture is thickened, 8-10 minutes.

Step 3: Stir in shrimp. Add sugar to taste; sprinkle with parsley. If desired, serve with spaghetti.

C. Nutrition Facts

1 cup shrimp mixture:
Calories: 228 Total Fat: 12g Total Carbohydrates: 8g Protein: 20g

Salmon and Spud Salad

| Cooking Information | | | | |

A. Ingredients

1 pound fingerling potatoes

1/2 pound fresh green beans

1/2 pound fresh asparagus

4 salmon fillets (6 ounces each)

1 tablespoon plus 1/3 cup red wine vinaigrette, divided

1/4 teaspoon salt

1/4 teaspoon pepper

4 cups fresh arugula or baby spinach

2 cups cherry tomatoes, halved

1 tablespoon minced fresh chives

B. Instructions

Step 1: Cut potatoes lengthwise in half. Trim and cut green beans and asparagus into 2-in. pieces.

Step 2: Place potatoes in a 6-qt. stockpot; add water to cover. Bring to a boil. Reduce heat; cook, uncovered, until tender, 10-15 minutes, adding green beans and asparagus during the last 4 minutes of cooking. Drain.

Step 3: Meanwhile, brush salmon with 1 tablespoon vinaigrette; sprinkle with salt and pepper. Place fish on oiled grill rack, skin side down. Grill, covered, over medium-high heat or broil 4 in. from heat until fish just begins to flake easily with a fork, 6-8 minutes.

Step 4: In a large bowl, combine potato mixture, arugula, tomatoes and chives. Drizzle with remaining vinaigrette; toss to coat. Serve with salmon.

C. Nutrition Facts

1 salmon fillet with 2 cups salad:
Calories: 480 Total Fat: 23g Total Carbohydrates: 33g Protein: 34g

Tomato-Poached Halibut

| Cooking Information | |

A. Ingredients

1 tablespoon olive oil
2 poblano peppers, finely chopped
1 small onion, finely chopped
1 can (14-1/2 ounces) fire-roasted diced tomatoes, undrained
1 can (14-1/2 ounces) no-salt-added diced tomatoes, undrained
1/4 cup chopped pitted green olives
3 garlic cloves, minced
1/4 teaspoon pepper
1/8 teaspoon salt
4 halibut fillets (4 ounces each)
1/3 cup chopped fresh cilantro
4 lemon wedges
Crusty whole grain bread, optional

B. Instructions

Step 1: In a large nonstick skillet, heat oil over medium-high heat.
Step 2: Add poblano peppers and onion; cook and stir 4-6 minutes or until tender.
Step 3: Stir in tomatoes, olives, garlic, pepper and salt. Bring to a boil. Adjust heat to maintain a gentle simmer.
Step 4: Add fillets. Cook, covered, 8-10 minutes or until fish just begins to flake easily with a fork. Sprinkle with cilantro.
Serve with lemon wedges and, if desired, bread.

C. Nutrition Facts

1 fillet with 1 cup sauce:
Calories: 224 Total Fat: 7g Total Carbohydrates: 17g Protein: 24g

A recipe has no soul unless you bring it to life.

Cilantro Lime Shrimp

| Cooking Information | | | | |

A. Ingredients

1/3 cup chopped fresh cilantro
1-1/2 teaspoons grated lime zest
1/3 cup lime juice
1 jalapeno pepper, seeded and minced
2 tablespoons olive oil
3 garlic cloves, minced
1/4 teaspoon salt
1/4 teaspoon ground cumin
1/4 teaspoon pepper
1 pound uncooked shrimp (16-20 per pound), peeled and deveined
Lime slices

B. Instructions

Step 1: Mix first 9 ingredients; toss with shrimp. Let stand 15 minutes.
Step 2: Thread shrimp and lime slices onto 4 metal or soaked wooden skewers.
Grill, covered, over medium heat until shrimp turn pink, 2-4 minutes per side.

C. Nutrition Facts

1 kabob:
Calories: 167
Total Fat: 8g
Total Carbohydrates: 4g
Protein: 19g

Split-Second Shrimp

| Cooking Information | 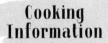 | | | | |

A. Ingredients

2 tablespoons butter

1 large garlic clove, minced

1/8 to 1/4 teaspoon cayenne pepper

2 tablespoons white wine or chicken broth

5 teaspoons lemon juice

1 tablespoon minced fresh parsley

1/2 teaspoon salt

1 pound uncooked shrimp (26-30 per pound), peeled and deveined

B. Instructions

Step 1: Place butter, garlic and cayenne in a 9-in. microwave-safe pie plate.

Step 2: Microwave, covered, on high until butter is melted, about 1 minute. Stir in wine, lemon juice, parsley and salt. Add shrimp; toss to coat.

Step 3: Microwave, covered, on high until shrimp turns pink, 2-1/2-3-1/2 minutes.
Stir before serving.

C. Nutrition Facts

3 ounces cooked shrimp:

Calories: 157

Total Fat: 7g

Total Carbohydrates: 2g

Protein: 19g

Citrus Scallops

Cooking Information				

A. Ingredients

1 medium green or sweet red pepper, julienned
4 green onions, chopped
1 garlic clove, minced
2 tablespoons olive oil
1 pound sea scallops
1/2 teaspoon salt
1/4 teaspoon crushed red pepper flakes
2 tablespoons lime juice
1/2 teaspoon grated lime zest
4 medium navel oranges, peeled and sectioned
2 teaspoons minced fresh cilantro
Hot cooked rice or pasta

B. Instructions

Step 1: In a large skillet, saute the pepper, onions and garlic in oil for 1 minute.
Step 2: Add scallops, salt and pepper flakes; cook for 4 minutes. Add lime juice and zest; cook for 1 minute.
Step 3: Reduce heat. Add orange sections and cilantro; cook 2 minutes longer or until scallops are opaque.
Serve with rice or pasta.

C. Nutrition Facts

1 serving (calculated without rice or pasta):
Calories: 240 Total Fat: 8g Total Carbohydrates: 23g Protein: 21g

Skinny Crab Quiche

A. Ingredients

1 can (6 ounces) crab
1-1/2 cups shredded reduced-fat cheddar cheese
1/2 cup shredded zucchini
1/3 cup chopped green onions
1-1/2 cups egg substitute
1 can (12 ounces) fat-free evaporated milk
3/4 teaspoon ground mustard
1/2 teaspoon salt
1/4 teaspoon salt-free lemon-pepper seasoning
Dash paprika

B. Instructions

Step 1: In a bowl, combine the crab, cheese, zucchini and onions. Press onto the bottom and up the sides of a 9-in. deep-dish pie plate coated with cooking spray.

Step 2: In another bowl, combine the egg substitute, milk, mustard, salt and lemon-pepper; mix well. Pour into crust. Sprinkle with paprika.

Step 3: Bake, uncovered, at 400° until a knife inserted in the center comes out clean, 25-30 minutes. Let stand for 10 minutes before cutting.

C. Nutrition Facts

1 slice:
Calories: 223
Total Fat: 9g
Total Carbohydrates: 10g
Protein: 26g

Cornmeal Catfish with Avocado Sauce

| Cooking Information | | | | |

A. Ingredients

1 medium ripe avocado, peeled and cubed

1/3 cup reduced-fat mayonnaise

1/4 cup fresh cilantro leaves

2 tablespoons lime juice

1/2 teaspoon garlic salt

1/4 cup cornmeal

1 teaspoon seafood seasoning

4 catfish fillets (6 ounces each)

3 tablespoons canola oil

1 medium tomato, chopped

B. Instructions

Step 1: Place the first 5 ingredients in a food processor; process until blended.

Step 2: In a shallow bowl, mix cornmeal and seafood seasoning. Dip catfish in cornmeal mixture to coat both sides; shake off excess.

Step 3: In a large skillet, heat oil over medium heat. Add catfish in batches; cook 4-5 minutes on each side or until fish flakes easily with a fork.

Step 4: Top with avocado sauce and chopped tomato.

C. Nutrition Facts

1 fillet with 3 tablespoons sauce:

Calories: 505

Total Fat: 37g

Total Carbohydrates: 15g

Protein: 29g

Lime Broiled Catfish

Cooking Information

A. Ingredients

1 tablespoon butter

2 tablespoons lime juice

1/2 teaspoon salt, optional

1/4 teaspoon pepper

1/4 teaspoon garlic powder

2 catfish fillets (6 ounces each)

Lime slices or wedges, optional

Fresh parsley, optional

B. Instructions

Step 1: Melt butter in a small saucepan. Stir in the lime juice, salt if desired, pepper and garlic powder. Remove from the heat and set aside.

Step 2: Place fillets in a shallow baking pan. Brush each fillet generously with lime-butter sauce. Broil for 5-8 minutes or until fish flakes easily with a fork.

Step 3: Remove to a warm serving dish; spoon pan juices over each fillet. Garnish with lime slices and parsley if desired.

C. Nutrition Facts

1 fillet:

Calories: 254

Total Fat: 14g

Total Carbohydrates: 2g

Protein: 31g

Southwestern Catfish

| Cooking Information | | | | |

A. Ingredients

3 medium tomatoes, chopped

1/4 cup chopped onion

2 jalapeno peppers, seeded and finely chopped

2 tablespoons white wine vinegar

3 teaspoons salt, divided

3 teaspoons paprika

3 teaspoons chili powder

1 to 1-1/2 teaspoons ground cumin

1 to 1-1/2 teaspoons ground coriander

3/4 to 1 teaspoon cayenne pepper

1/2 teaspoon garlic powder

4 catfish fillets (6 ounces each)

B. Instructions

Step 1: For salsa, in a large bowl, combine the tomatoes, onion, jalapenos, vinegar and 1 teaspoon salt. Cover and refrigerate for at least 30 minutes.

Step 2: Combine the paprika, chili powder, cumin, coriander, cayenne, garlic powder and remaining salt; rub over catfish.

Step 3: Using long-handled tongs, moisten a paper towel with cooking oil and lightly coat the grill rack.

Step 4: Grill fillets, uncovered, over medium heat or broil 4 in. from the heat for 5 minutes on each side or until fish flakes easily with a fork. Serve with salsa.

C. Nutrition Facts

Per serving:
Calories: 107 Total Fat: 4g Total Carbohydrates: 10g Protein: 9g

Breaded Sea Scallops

Cooking Information

A. Ingredients

1 large egg
1/3 cup mashed potato flakes
1/3 cup seasoned bread crumbs
1/8 teaspoon salt
1/8 teaspoon pepper
6 sea scallops (about 3/4 pound)
2 tablespoons all-purpose flour
2 tablespoons butter
1 tablespoon canola oil

B. Instructions

Step 1: In a shallow bowl, lightly beat egg.

Step 2: In another bowl, toss potato flakes and bread crumbs with salt and pepper. In a third bowl, toss scallops with flour to coat lightly.

Dip in egg, then in potato mixture, patting to adhere.

Step 3: In a large skillet, heat butter and oil over medium heat.

Add scallops; cook until golden brown and scallops are firm and opaque, 2-3 minutes per side.

C. Nutrition Facts

3 scallops:
Calories: 453
Total Fat: 23g
Total Carbohydrates: 33g
Protein: 28g

Secret Ingredient Fried Catfish

| Cooking Information | | | | |

A. Ingredients

2 eggs
2 tablespoons carbonated water
1 cup pancake mix
1/2 teaspoon seasoned salt
1/4 teaspoon pepper
4 catfish fillets (6 ounces each)
Oil for deep-fat frying

B. Instructions

Step 1: In a shallow bowl, whisk eggs and water.
Step 2: In another shallow bowl, combine the pancake mix, seasoned salt and pepper. Dip fillets in egg mixture, then coat with seasoned pancake mix.
Step 3: In an electric skillet or deep-fat fryer, heat oil to 375°. Fry fillets, a few at a time, for 2-3 minutes or until golden brown. Drain on paper towels.

C. Nutrition Facts

1 fillet:
Calories: 475
Total Fat: 34g
Total Carbohydrates: 10g
Protein: 29g

Shrimp & Avocado Salad

| Cooking Information | | | | | |

A. Ingredients

1 pound large peeled, deveined cooked shrimp, coarsely chopped

3 small ripe avocados, cubed

½ cup thinly sliced radishes

¼ cup thinly sliced scallions

¼ cup extra-virgin olive oil

¼ cup fresh lime juice

1 tablespoon grated fresh ginger

2 teaspoons granulated sugar

¾ teaspoon salt

¼ teaspoon crushed red pepper

12 cups mixed greens or chopped romaine lettuce

Chopped fresh cilantro for garnish

B. Instructions

Step 1: Gently stir shrimp, avocados, radishes and scallions together in a medium bowl. Step 2: Whisk oil, lime juice, ginger, sugar, salt and crushed red pepper in a small bowl. Step 3: Pour the dressing over the shrimp mixture; gently stir to coat well.

Step 4: Divide greens (or lettuce) among 6 plates; top evenly with the shrimp mixture and garnish with cilantro, if desired.

C. Nutrition Facts

Per serving:
Calories: 367 Total Fat: 25g Total Carbohydrates: 17g Protein: 21g

Linguine with Creamy White Clam Sauce

| Cooking Information | | | | |

A. Ingredients

8 ounces whole-wheat linguine

1 16-ounce container chopped clams or two 10-ounce cans whole baby clams

3 tablespoons extra-virgin olive oil

3 cloves garlic, chopped

¼ teaspoon crushed red pepper

1 tablespoon lemon juice

¼ teaspoon salt

1 large tomato, chopped

¼ cup chopped fresh basil, plus more for garnish

2 tablespoons heavy cream or half-and-half

B. Instructions

Step 1: Bring a large saucepan of water to a boil. Add pasta and cook until just tender, about 8 minutes or according to package directions. Drain.

Step 2: Meanwhile, drain clams, reserving 3/4 cup of the liquid. Heat oil in a large skillet over medium-high heat.

Step 3: Add garlic and crushed red pepper and cook, stirring, for 30 seconds. Add the reserved clam liquid, lemon juice and salt; bring to a simmer and cook until slightly reduced, 2 to 3 minutes.

Step 4: Add tomato and the clams; bring to a simmer and cook for 1 minute more. Remove from heat.

Step 5: Stir in basil and cream (or half-and-half). Add the pasta and toss to coat with the sauce. Garnish with more basil, if desired.

C. Nutrition Facts

Per serving:
Calories: 421 Total Fat: 17g Total Carbohydrates: 52g Protein: 22g

A recipe has no soul unless you bring it to life.

Creamy One-Pot Penne Primavera with Shrimp

| Cooking Information | | | | | |

A. Ingredients

8 ounces whole-wheat penne pasta

5 cloves garlic, sliced

4 cups water

2 cups broccoli florets

1 small red bell pepper, diced

½ teaspoon kosher salt

¼ teaspoon ground pepper

⅔ cup grated Parmesan cheese

12 ounces shrimp, shelled, deveined and cut into halves or thirds

4 cups baby spinach

1 ½ cups cherry tomatoes, halved

B. Instructions

Step 1: Combine pasta, garlic and water in a large, high-sided skillet. Bring to a boil over medium-high heat; reduce heat to maintain a gentle boil and cook, stirring frequently, for 8 minutes.

Step 2: Add broccoli, bell pepper, salt and pepper; cook, stirring often, until the vegetables and pasta are tender, about 5 minutes more. Reduce heat to low and add Parmesan a few tablespoons at a time, tossing the pasta between each addition until well coated.

Step 3: Stir in shrimp and spinach; cook, tossing constantly, until the spinach is wilted and the shrimp is cooked through, about 5 minutes. Remove from heat and stir in tomatoes. Serve immediately.

C. Nutrition Facts

Per serving:
Calories: 373 Total Fat: 6g Total Carbohydrates: 52g Protein: 32g

Tuna Poke

Cooking Information

A. Ingredients

¾ cup thinly sliced scallion greens

¼ cup reduced-sodium tamari

1 ½ tablespoons mirin

1 ½ tablespoons toasted (dark) sesame oil

1 tablespoon toasted sesame seeds

2 teaspoons grated fresh ginger

½ teaspoon crushed red pepper (Optional)

12 ounces sushi-grade tuna, skinned and cut into 1/2-inch cubes

2 cups cooked brown rice

2 tablespoons rice vinegar

2 cups sliced snow peas

2 cups sliced cucumber

¼ cup chopped chives

B. Instructions

Step 1: Whisk scallion greens, tamari, mirin, oil, sesame seeds, ginger and crushed red pepper, if using, in a medium bowl.

Step 2: Set aside 2 tablespoons of the sauce in a small bowl. Add tuna to the sauce in the medium bowl and gently toss to coat.

Step 3: Combine rice and vinegar in a large bowl. Divide among 4 bowls and top each with 3/4 cup tuna, 1/2 cup each snow peas and cucumber, and 1 tablespoon each chives and furikake.

Step 4: Drizzle with the reserved sauce and serve.

C. Nutrition Facts

Per serving:
Calories: 371 Total Fat: 11g Total Carbohydrates: 39g Protein: 26g

A recipe has no soul unless you bring it to life.

Slow-Cooker Spicy Mussels in Tomato-Fennel Ragu

| Cooking Information | | | | |

A. Ingredients

1 tablespoon olive oil

1 fennel bulb, thinly sliced, fronds reserved for garnish

1 yellow onion , chopped

1 carrot, chopped

1 celery stalk, chopped

3 garlic cloves, smashed

¾ cup dry white wine

2 tomatoes, roughly chopped

2 bay leaves

1 lemon, halved

¾ teaspoon kosher salt

½ teaspoon crushed red pepper

2 pounds small mussels, scrubbed and debearded

B. Instructions

Step 1: Heat oil in a skillet over medium-high heat. Add fennel, onion, carrot, celery and cook 8 minutes. Add garlic and cook 2 minutes. Add wine, reduce 4-5 minutes.

Step 2: Transfer to slow cooker. Stir in tomatoes, bay leaves, lemon halves, salt and red pepper. Cook 3 hours.

Step 3: Add mussels and cook 30-40 minutes until opened. Discard bay leaves, lemons and any unopened mussels.

Step 4: Cook linguine omitting salt and fat. Divide pasta, mussels and sauce between bowls. Garnish with fennel fronds if desired.

C. Nutrition Facts

Per serving:
Calories: 453 Total Fat: 7g Total Carbohydrates: 57g Protein: 44g

Clam Pizza Fra Diavolo

A. Ingredients

1 1/4-1 1/2 cups self-rising flour (see Tips)

1 cup low-fat plain Greek yogurt

2 tablespoons extra-virgin olive oil

2 tablespoons jarred chopped Calabrian peppers (see Tips)

2 cloves garlic, finely grated

1 cup chopped broccoli florets

1 (6.5 ounce) can chopped clams, drained

4 ounces fresh mozzarella, patted dry and torn into bite-size pieces

2 tablespoons grated Parmesan cheese

Chopped fresh parsley for garnish

B. Instructions

Step 1: Preheat oven to 450°F with racks in upper and lower thirds. Dust a baking sheet with flour.

Step 2: Mix 1 1/4 cups self-rising flour and yogurt on low speed until a smooth dough forms, adding more flour as needed. Roll into a 12-inch circle on floured surface and transfer to baking sheet.

Step 3: Toss peppers and garlic with oil. Spread 3 tbsp of mixture over crust. Toss broccoli with remaining mixture and scatter over pizza with clams and mozzarella.

Step 4: Bake on lower rack 13-16 minutes until underside is golden brown. Move to upper rack and broil 1-2 minutes until cheese is bubbly and crust is browned.

Let cool 5 minutes. Garnish with Parmesan and parsley if desired.

C. Nutrition Facts

Per serving:
Calories: 327 Total Fat: 13g Total Carbohydrates: 29g Protein: 18g

Tuna Casserole with Orzo, Eggplant & Feta

| Cooking Information | | | | |

A. Ingredients

8oz orzo pasta

1 medium eggplant, diced

1 onion, diced

3 garlic cloves, minced

2 cans (5oz) tuna, drained

1 cup marinara sauce

½ cup crumbled feta cheese

¼ cup fresh parsley, chopped

2 tbsp olive oil

Salt and pepper

B. Instructions

Step 1: Preheat oven to 375°F. Grease a casserole dish and set aside.

Step 2: Cook orzo pasta according to package instructions. Drain and transfer to casserole dish.

Step 3: In a skillet over medium heat, sauté eggplant, onion and garlic with olive oil for 5 minutes until softened. Season with salt and pepper.

Step 4: Add eggplant mixture to casserole dish along with tuna, marinara sauce and feta cheese. Mix well and bake for 20 minutes.

Step 5: Top with fresh parsley before serving.

C. Nutrition Facts

Per serving:
Calories: 239
Total Fat: 8g
Total Carbohydrates: 24g
Protein: 20g

Garlic Butter–Roasted Salmon with Potatoes & Asparagus

| Cooking Information | | |

A. Ingredients

1 pound baby Yukon Gold potatoes, halved

2 tablespoons extra-virgin olive oil, divided

¾ teaspoon salt, divided

½ teaspoon ground pepper, divided

12 ounces asparagus, trimmed

2 tablespoons melted butter

1 tablespoon lemon juice

2 cloves garlic, minced

1 ¼ pounds salmon fillet, skinned and cut into 4 portions

Chopped parsley for garnish

B. Instructions

Step 1: Preheat oven to 400°F. Toss potatoes, 1 tablespoon oil, 1/4 teaspoon salt and 1/8 teaspoon pepper together in a medium bowl. Spread in an even layer on a large rimmed baking sheet. Roast until starting to soften and brown, about 15 minutes.

Step 2: Meanwhile, toss asparagus with the remaining 1 tablespoon oil, 1/8 teaspoon salt and 1/8 teaspoon pepper in the medium bowl. Combine butter, lemon juice, garlic, 1/4 teaspoon salt and the remaining 1/4 teaspoon pepper in a small bowl.

Step 3: Sprinkle salmon with the remaining 1/8 teaspoon salt. Move the potatoes to one side of the pan. Place the salmon in the center of the pan; drizzle with the butter mixture. Spread the asparagus on the empty side of the pan. Roast until the salmon is just cooked through and the vegetables are tender, 10 to 12 minutes. Garnish with parsley.

C. Nutrition Facts

Per serving:
Calories: 522 Total Fat: 32g Total Carbohydrates: 26g Protein: 34g

Salmon & Avocado Salad

Cooking Information

A. Ingredients

½ cup loosely packed fresh dill, plus more for garnish
2 tablespoons water
2 tablespoons lemon juice
2 tablespoons white-wine vinegar
1 teaspoon Dijon mustard
1 small clove garlic
2 avocados, chopped, divided
¼ cup extra-virgin olive oil, plus 1 teaspoon, divided
½ teaspoon salt, divided
4 (5 ounce) skinless salmon fillets
¼ teaspoon ground pepper
3 cups spring mix salad greens
2 cups thinly sliced red cabbage

B. Instructions

Step 1: Make dressing by blending dill, water, lemon juice, vinegar, mustard, garlic, 1/2 avocado, 1/4 oil and 1/4 tsp salt. Refrigerate.

Step 2: Heat 1 tsp oil in skillet over medium-high heat. Season salmon with pepper and 1/4 tsp salt.

Step 3: Cook 4 minutes until golden brown and mostly opaque at sides. Flip fillets, remove from heat and let stand 2-3 minutes until cooked through.

Step 4: Toss salad greens, cabbage, carrots with reserved dressing. Divide among plates and top with remaining avocado.

Step 5: Add salmon fillet on top. Garnish with extra dill if desired.

C. Nutrition Facts

Per serving:
Calories: 508 Total Fat: 36g Total Carbohydrates: 13g Protein: 35g

Lemony Linguine with Spring Vegetables

Cooking Information					

A. Ingredients

8 ounces whole-wheat linguine or fettuccine

4 cloves garlic, thinly sliced

½ teaspoon salt

¼ teaspoon ground pepper

3 ½ cups water

1 9-ounce package frozen artichoke hearts

6 cups chopped mature spinach

2 cups peas, fresh or frozen

½ cup grated Parmesan cheese, divided

¼ cup half-and-half

1 tablespoon lemon zest

3-4 tablespoons lemon juice

B. Instructions

Step 1: Combine pasta, garlic, salt and pepper in a large pot. Add water. Bring to a boil over high heat. Boil, stirring frequently, for 8 minutes.

Step 2: Stir in artichokes, spinach and peas and cook until the pasta is tender and the water has almost evaporated, 2 to 4 minutes more.

Step 3: Remove from heat and stir in 1/4 cup cheese, half-and-half, lemon zest and lemon juice to taste. Let stand, stirring occasionally, for 5 minutes.

Serve sprinkled with the remaining 1/4 cup cheese.

C. Nutrition Facts

Per serving:
Calories: 372
Total Fat: 7g
Total Carbohydrates: 64g

A recipe has no soul unless you bring it to life.

Scallops & Spring Vegetables with Olive–Caper Pan Sauce

Cooking Information |

A. Ingredients

2 tablespoons extra-virgin olive oil, divided

8 ounces dry sea scallops, tough side muscle removed

Pinch of ground pepper

8 ounces asparagus (1/2 bunch), trimmed

6 ounces petite carrots, trimmed or baby carrots, halved lengthwise

1 medium shallot, minced

5 pitted Castelvetrano olives, coarsely chopped

1 tablespoon capers, rinsed and chopped

1 clove garlic, minced

¼ cup dry white wine

1 tablespoon butter

Chopped fresh parsley for garnish

B. Instructions

Step 1: Heat 1 tablespoon oil in a medium nonstick skillet over medium-high heat. Pat scallops dry and sprinkle with pepper.

Step 2: Add the scallops to the pan and cook, flipping once, until browned and just cooked through, 1 1/2 to 2 minutes per side. Transfer to a plate.

Step 3: Add the remaining 1 tablespoon oil, asparagus and carrots to the pan and cook, stirring frequently, until tender-crisp, 2 to 3 minutes. Add shallot, olives, capers and garlic and cook until fragrant, about 1 minute. Add wine and cook for 1 minute.

Step 4: Remove from heat and add butter; stir until melted. Serve with the scallops, sprinkled with parsley, if desired.

C. Nutrition Facts

Per serving:
Calories: 384 Total Fat: 22g Total Carbohydrates: 24g Protein: 18g

Tuscan Tuna with Tomato Salad

| Cooking Information | | | | |

A. Ingredients

4 (5 to 6 ounce) fresh or frozen tuna steaks, about 1-inch thick

3 teaspoons white wine vinegar, divided

1 teaspoon olive oil

½ teaspoon dried Italian seasoning, crushed

¼ teaspoon salt

½ teaspoon ground pepper, divided

2 medium tomatoes, seeded and chopped (1 cup)

½ cup thinly sliced fennel bulb

¼ cup chopped fresh basil

1 medium shallot, halved and thinly sliced

1 clove garlic, minced

1 tablespoon pine nuts, toasted (see Tip) and chopped

1 tablespoon grated Parmesan cheese

B. Instructions

Step 1: Thaw fish if frozen. Rinse, pat dry. Brush tuna with oil mixture of 1 tsp vinegar, olive oil, Italian seasoning, salt and 1/4 tsp pepper.

Step 2: In a bowl, make tomato salad by mixing tomatoes, fennel, basil, shallot, garlic, remaining 2 tsp vinegar and 1/4 tsp pepper.

Step 3: For charcoal grill, place tuna over medium coals. Grill uncovered 6-8 minutes, turning once, until fish flakes easily with a fork.

Step 4: Serve tuna with tomato salad. Sprinkle with pine nuts and Parmesan.

C. Nutrition Facts

Per serving:
Calories: 256 Total Fat: 10g Total Carbohydrates: 5g Protein: 35g

Spaghetti with Arugula & Clam Sauce

| Cooking Information | | | | |

A. Ingredients

8 ounces whole-wheat spaghetti (see Tip)
2 tablespoons extra-virgin olive oil
½ cup chopped onion
4 cloves garlic, thinly sliced
¼ teaspoon crushed red pepper
1 (10 ounce) can whole clams
¼ cup dry white wine
Zest and juice of 1 lemon
1 tablespoon butter
⅛ teaspoon salt
4 cups baby arugula
Grated Parmesan cheese (Optional)

B. Instructions

Step 1: Bring a large pot of water to a boil. Cook pasta according to package directions. Drain.

Step 2: Meanwhile, heat oil in a large skillet over medium heat. Add onion and cook until starting to soften, about 2 minutes. Add garlic and crushed red pepper and cook, stirring, until fragrant, about 1 minute. Add clams and their juice, wine, lemon zest and lemon juice. Bring to a simmer.

Step 3: Adjust heat to maintain a simmer and cook, stirring occasionally, until reduced by half, 6 to 8 minutes.

Step 4: Stir in butter and salt. Add the hot pasta and toss to coat. Add arugula and toss until slightly wilted, about 1 minute.

Serve with Parmesan, if desired.

C. Nutrition Facts

Per serving:
Calories: 397
Total Fat: 14g
Total Carbohydrates: 50g
Protein: 21g

Thank you for choosing The 30-Minute Pescatarian Cookbook. We hope that this cookbook has provided you with valuable information and delicious recipes to support your journey towards a healthier lifestyle.
Whether you're just starting out or already have some kitchen skills, remember that practice makes progress.
We're so glad you joined us on this tasty journey. Your support means so much, and we hope these recipes bring you joy and satisfaction.
Let us know if you have any other questions - we're always here to help fellow food lovers like you.
Happy cooking and enjoy your nutrition meals!